spot

SPORTS

FIGURE SKATING

by Mari Schuh

AMICUS | AMICUS INK

Zamboni

costume

Look for these words and pictures as you read.

judges

blade

A figure skater spins.
See her go!

Some skaters skate alone.
Others skate in pairs.
Let's watch!

Do you see the Zamboni?
It smooths the ice.
Now the ice rink is ready!

Zamboni

Do you see the costume?
It is made of spandex.
It stretches.
It lets the skater move.

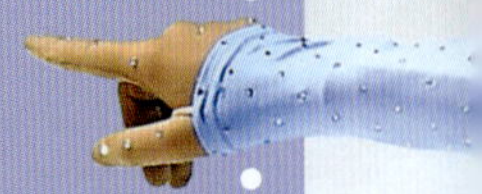

costume

Do you see the judges?
They score each move.
Hard moves earn more points.

judges

Do you see the blade?
The toe pick is at the front.
It grabs the ice.
A skater can jump high!

blade

Watch him do a camel spin.
He sticks out one leg. Nice job!

Zamboni

costume

Did you find?

judges

blade

Spot is published by Amicus and Amicus Ink
P.O. Box 1329, Mankato, MN 56002
www.amicuspublishing.us

Library of Congress Cataloging-in-Publication Data
Names: Schuh, Mari C., 1975- author.
Title: Figure skating / by Mari Schuh.
Description: Mankato, MN : Amicus, 2020. | Series: Spot. Sports | Audience: K to Grade 3.
Identifiers: LCCN 2018037237 (print) | LCCN 2018037742 (ebook) | ISBN 9781681517322 (pdf) | ISBN 9781681516509 (library binding) | ISBN 9781681524368 (pbk.)
Subjects: LCSH: Figure skating--Juvenile literature. | Picture puzzles--Juvenile literature.
Classification: LCC GV850.4 (ebook) | LCC GV850.4 .S377 2020 (print) | DDC 796.91/2--dc23
LC record available at https://lccn.loc.gov/2018037237

Printed in China

HC 10 9 8 7 6 5 4 3 2 1
PB 10 9 8 7 6 5 4 3 2 1

For Natalie of Fairmont, Minnesota —MS

Wendy Dieker, editor
Deb Miner, series designer
Aubrey Harper, book designer
Holly Young, photo researcher

Photos by Ivan Sekretarev/AP cover, 16; Roma Barelko/Shutterstock 1; Wildcow/iStock 3; Richard Wareham Fotografie/Alamy 4–5; PCN Photography/Alamy 6–7; Tom Dulat/Stringer/Getty 8–9; Roberto Schmidt/Getty 10–11; dimamorgan12/iStock 12–13; Leonard Zhukovsky/Shutterstock 14–15